Money Pillars

Your Path To Abundant Wealth

Ronald V. Moore

Money Pillars

Copyright

Copyright © 2024, 2025 by Ronald V. Moore. All rights reserved.

This revised edition was published in 2025. No part of this publication may be reproduced, distributed, or transmitted in any form or by any means, including photocopying, recording, or other electronic or mechanical methods, without the prior written permission of the publisher or author, except in the case of brief quotations used in critical reviews or scholarly articles.

This book is intended for educational and informational purposes only. It does not constitute financial, legal, or professional advice. Readers should consult qualified professionals before making any financial decisions.

Money Pillars

Contents

Money Pillars

Copyright

Introduction

Chapter 1

Foundation for Financial Success

Chapter 2

Creating a Wealth-Oriented Mentality

Chapter 3

Investment Strategies

Chapter 4

Building Wealth Using Real Estate

Chapter 5

Debt Management

Chapter 6

Income Streams

Money Pillars

Chapter 7

Savings Blueprint

Chapter 8

Risk Management: Protecting Your Wealth

Chapter 9

Creating Wealth Through Entrepreneurship

Chapter 10

Legacy Planning: Protecting Your Wealth for Future Generations

Conclusion

Introduction

There comes a moment—quiet, private, often painful—when you realize something isn't working. You work hard. You stay up late. You sacrifice. But your bank account doesn't reflect your effort. Your dreams feel too expensive. And the future? Unclear. Unstable. Maybe even out of reach.

That moment is where Money Pillars begins.

This book was written for people like you—smart, capable, resilient people—who've been left out of the wealth conversation for far too long. People who only learned how to seek money, not how to create it. People who've been told to "budget harder," "grind more," or "stop buying coffee," but never shown what real, lasting wealth actually looks like—or how to build it from the ground up.

Money Pillars

You see, wealth isn't about luck. It's not reserved for the elite, or the Ivy League, or the ones born into the right zip code. Wealth is built—quietly, consistently, with intention. And the truth no one tells you? You can start exactly where you are. You don't need to be perfect. You don't need thousands in the bank. You don't even need to know everything.

You just need a better foundation.

Money Pillars is that foundation.

This book is not theory. It's not motivational fluff. It's not another list of "10 ways to get rich." It's a system—a set of unshakable financial pillars designed to give you clarity, control, and confidence with money.

Each chapter gives you something solid to stand on: a mindset shift, a proven strategy, a tool that works in the real world. You'll learn how money flows, how wealth grows, and how to stop surviving and start building wealth. We'll unpack the emotional weight of financial struggle and replace it with structure, power, and peace of mind.

Because you deserve more than just "getting by."

You deserve to wake up without worrying about your bills. You deserve to walk into a store and not flinch at the price tag. You deserve to invest in your future—not just wish for one. You deserve to break the cycle of scarcity and step into a life that feels abundant, grounded, and yours.

And yes, it's possible.

Wealth is not a finish line—it's a path. And you're not late. You're not too far gone. You haven't missed your shot. You're about to make a big choice. Right here. Right now.

Money Pillars

No matter your income. No matter your history. No matter how many financial mistakes or detours you've taken—this is where everything can start to change.

But not by accident.

By design.

So, if you're ready to stop guessing. If you are tired of the fear, confusion, and pressure. If you're done watching others "make it" while you wonder what you're missing.

You're in the right place.

This is not just a book. It's a rebuild. A reset. A financial awakening.

One pillar at a time, we'll take back what's yours: your power, your peace, and your future.

Let's begin.

Money Pillars

Chapter 1

Foundation for Financial Success

You can't thrive when money keeps you up at night. Not when rent is due, debt is growing, or unexpected bills hit without warning. The truth is—peace of mind isn't only a feeling. It's rooted in financial stability.

A fulfilling life—one where you feel free, focused, and able to be your best self—rests on something we don't talk about enough: a solid financial base. Not massive wealth. Not luxury. Just stability.

Good financial health doesn't happen by chance. It takes clear planning, small habits, and a mindset shift. And when you get it right, everything improves: your relationships, your work, even your mental health.

This chapter gives you exactly what you need to take action. No fluff. No guesswork. Just clear, practical steps to help you feel confident—and calm—about your money.

What a Financial Foundation Really Is

Your financial life is the surface every decision stands on—if it's unstable, even your best plans can collapse. If it's solid, you walk tall, take risks, and plan ahead. If it's cracked, every step feels uncertain. Your financial foundation isn't just about numbers. It takes shape through your daily choices—purposeful saving, conscious spending, and a clear, steady approach to budgeting.

Money Pillars

These are the tools that shape your future, protect your peace of mind, and allow you to take care of what matters most.

Without this foundation, life gets shaky. Bills pile up. Goals get delayed. And worse—stress starts to seep into everything: your health, your work, even your relationships.

Here's the reality: Nearly half of Americans—44%—can't cover an unexpected $400 expense. That's not just a statistic. That's millions of people living one emergency away from disaster. And more than 38% of families carry credit card debt that keeps growing—because income alone isn't enough without structure.

Even people earning decent wages often feel stuck—working hard, yet still trapped in a cycle of anxiety, debt, and financial instability. Living paycheck to paycheck isn't always about laziness or lack of ambition. It's often about not having the right tools or guidance.

Financial stress doesn't just stay in your wallet. It shows up in your sleep, your mood, your decisions—and in the lives of those around you.

The Five Key Components of Your Financial Foundation

Earning a steady paycheck. Signing the lease on a space that finally feels like yours. Closing on your first home. These are big moments—important steps in building a life. But by themselves, they're not enough to keep you financially secure. A job and a place to live give you structure, but not stability. Real financial strength comes from what you build beneath those milestones—the habits, systems, and choices that quietly hold everything together.

What comes next are the essential pieces that form that foundation.

1. Budgeting: Budgeting Isn't Optional. It's Survival with Intention: Money slips through your hands fast—especially when you're not paying attention. If you don't name your money's job, it'll find its own. Usually, it won't work out well for you. A budget isn't just numbers on paper. It's a tool to help you breathe easier, stop the chaos, and finally feel in control of what you've worked so hard to earn.

So let's cut the fluff. Here's how to build a budget that actually works—for your real life.

Step 1: Count Only What Actually Shows Up: What's your true monthly income? Not what you were promised. Not what's "on paper." We're talking about what actually lands in your hands after taxes, fees, or delays.

Side hustles? Add them in only if they're regular. Gifts or windfalls? Leave those out. Start with your real number.

Step 2: List the Money That Must Leave:

Now write down the payments you can't skip—ever.

This is your "keep life running" list. The roof over your head. Lights. Water. Transportation. Any loan or debt you can't miss without consequences.

You're not guessing here. Pull out bills. Look at last month's statements. Know exactly where every dollar goes.

Step 3: Find the Silent Drains:

This is where most people fall off. The small, daily, "I deserve this" expenses.

Look at your last two weeks. Be honest. Every snack, stream, ride, scroll-buy.

Write them down. See them for what they are—not shame, just data. You're not judging, you're tracking. You're reclaiming your awareness.

Step 4: Give Every Category a Boundary:

You're the boss now. Look at what you spend vs. what you earn. Is it adding up? Or bleeding over?

Start trimming—not slashing. One fewer outing. A pause on subscriptions. Swap brands. Give each category a clear ceiling. Choose numbers that feel realistic—not punishing.

This is where freedom begins. In boundaries, not in burnout.

Step 5: Leave Space for Sanity and Safety:
Nobody sticks to a budget that feels like punishment. You need a little space to breathe. So leave room for something that makes you smile—yes, even if money's tight. A coffee, a movie, a small escape. Then quietly build your cushion. $5, $50, whatever you can. The amount doesn't matter. The habit does. Build the habit now—your future self will thank you.

Step 6: Watch the Flow, Don't Forget the Plan:
Each week, glance at your spending. Once a month, sit down and check:

- Did you stick to it?

- Where did things go off course?
- What can you adjust for next month?

Life moves. Your budget should move with it. Don't aim for perfection. Aim for rhythm.

This Isn't Restriction. It's Rescue.
A budget is a blueprint for freedom, not a means of punishment. It shows you what's possible. It gives you room to breathe. It makes space for growth, security, peace—and the version of you that doesn't flinch when money comes up. You don't have to get it right all at once. But you do have to start.

2. Emergency Funds: A Cushion You Can't Afford to Skip: Consider a Monday morning when your automobile won't start. The mechanic says it'll cost you $700 to fix. Or worse—someone in your household ends up in the emergency room. One unexpected expense like that, and you're in crisis—unless you've built a buffer.

That buffer is your emergency fund. It's not a luxury. It's not something "extra." It's your first line of defense when life throws the unexpected. And life will throw the unexpected.

Start small—really small if you have to. If you can set aside just $20 per week, that's $1,040 after a year. Keep that money in a separate account you don't touch for day-to-day spending. Automate the transfer if possible. Out of sight, out of temptation.

Don't get hung up on the "three to six months" rule right away. That's a long-term goal. First, aim to cover one month's worth of bare-bones expenses—rent, food, transportation, and utilities. Once that feels manageable, move on to two months. Then three. Progress, not perfection, is what matters here.

Your emergency fund should sit in a liquid, easy-to-access account—like a high-yield savings account or even a basic savings account with no fees. Don't tie this money up in investments. You want to be able to reach it immediately if something goes wrong.

3. Short-Term Savings: Planning, Not Panicking: Let's say you want to travel next summer. Or your laptop is nearing the end of its life. These aren't emergencies, but they are future costs. Plan ahead by setting specific savings objectives rather than using your credit card or emergency fund.

Open a second savings account (or even a digital "goal" within your banking app). Label it:

"Vacation Fund," "Laptop Fund," "Christmas 2025." Then divide the total cost by the number of months until you need it. For example:

Do you want to spend $600 on a trip in six months? That's $100/month.

Need a $1,200 laptop by year's end? Save $150/month for the next eight months.

Make it automatic. Let your bank move the money the day you get paid—before you spend anything else.

Don't underestimate the power of small, regular deposits. Even saving $10 every week adds up to over $500 a year. That's half a plane ticket—or one less emergency on your credit card.

4. Real Investments: Start Slow, Stay Smart: Once you've built your emergency fund and have savings habits in place, you can start thinking long-term. That's where investing comes in.

You may begin without having a lot of money. You don't need to be an expert either. What you do need is patience, discipline, and a clear goal.

Begin with what you can afford to lose. That might be $25 a month. Many platforms let you start investing with almost nothing—apps like Fidelity, Vanguard, or even Acorns and Robinhood (depending on your country). Set up automatic monthly contributions and forget about trying to "time the market." That's gambling. You're building.

Start with index funds or ETFs (Exchange-Traded Funds). These are baskets of stocks that spread your risk across dozens or hundreds of companies. They're lower-cost and more stable than betting on individual stocks.

Money Pillars

Be cautious of hype. If the promise of "doubling your money in three months" seems too good to be true, it is. Stick with slow, boring, long-term growth. That's how real wealth builds.

If your employer offers a retirement account, like a 401(k), enroll immediately—especially if they match contributions. That's free money. Always try to provide enough to win the entire game. If they offer a Roth 401(k), and you expect to be in a higher tax bracket later, that may be even better—your withdrawals in retirement are tax-free.

If you're self-employed or freelancing, look into options like an IRA, Roth IRA, or SEP IRA depending on your income level. You don't have to wait to begin until you're "earning more." You need to start now, with what you've got.

How to Build a Strong Financial Foundation

You don't need a six-figure salary or decades of savings to start building a strong financial foundation. Whether you've just landed your first job or you've been working for years, your current position in life doesn't limit your ability to take control. The turning point isn't when you have more—it's when you choose to begin with what's already in your hands.

Financial planning isn't reserved for the wealthy. While the spotlight often shines on high-end advisors and investment managers, there are countless certified financial planners and money coaches who focus on helping everyday people build healthy financial habits—step by step, from the ground up.

Think of it like building a house. You can't just stack bricks and hope for the best. You need footings, a strong foundation wall, and a level base. Money works the same way. A lasting financial life starts with structure—built intentionally, one piece at a time. What follows are the tools to help you lay that foundation: practical, real-world techniques designed to support your stability, growth, and peace of mind.

Get Your Affairs in Order: Before a single brick is laid, before concrete is poured, any builder starts with the basics: the ground, the materials, the blueprint. Nothing solid can rise without first knowing what's there—and what's missing. Your financial foundation is no different. Before you can build wealth, security, or freedom, you need to know exactly what you're working with.

Money Pillars

That means taking full inventory—not just of what you hope to have, but of what you actually own right now.

Write it all down. Every asset.

Think beyond your bank account. What's the resale value of your car? Do you own a home or land? Jewelry with appraised value? Retirement funds, investment accounts, collectibles—anything you could convert to cash, even in a pinch. Be honest. Be thorough. This isn't about judgment. It's about clarity.

Then comes the part most people want to avoid: your liabilities.

What do you owe? Student loans, credit card balances, unpaid bills, car loans, personal debts—gather every number. Don't round down. Don't skip the small stuff. It adds up. And you deserve to know exactly how.

Money Pillars

After listing all your assets and debts, subtract what you owe from what you own.

That number is your net worth. But let's be clear: it's not your worth as a person. It's not a score. It's just a snapshot—a single data point that shows you where you stand financially, right now. Whether it's high, low, or even in the red, this number matters because it's honest. And honesty is your greatest leverage. Every journey—financial or otherwise—begins with a single step. And that step is knowing where you're standing.

This is your baseline.

Your launching point.

Your home ground.

You can't design a future until you've named your present. And this step—this full, unflinching view—is how you reclaim control.

Not someday. Not when things "get better." Right now.

So start with what you have. Know what you owe. And see the real picture.

Because no financial journey begins in theory. It begins here—with what's real.

Set Long-Term Goals: When constructing a structure's foundation, the design is carefully considered. In the same vein, your financial foundation must be specifically designed to support your long-term objectives. This includes making specific plans for your savings. For example, money set aside outside of an emergency fund can be strategically allocated to achieve a specific goal. Your goal could be to save for a down payment on a house, to pay for your children's education, or to fund a major life event such as a wedding. Clearly defined goals are powerful motivators that help keep your savings efforts on track.

A solid financial foundation isn't just about what you have now—it's also about what you're building toward. Creating a clear, actionable plan for increasing your income can make a powerful difference. That might mean developing new skills, pursuing growth in your current career, or launching a side project that brings in extra cash. Each step toward additional income expands your options and adds strength to your financial base. And just as important, you need a plan for the season when work is no longer your main source of income. Think about when you'd like to retire and what kind of life you want to lead. Then work backward. How much will you need saved, invested, or flowing in through passive income to support that future?

That long-range clarity brings sharper focus to the choices you're making right now.

Prioritize Strategies to Protect Yourself: Your financial foundation must achieve at least two primary goals: financial security and stability. This necessitates the implementation of strong safeguards to protect your financial life from unforeseen shocks. Emergency savings provide obvious, immediate benefits in the face of unexpected events. Job uncertainty, for example, can be a major source of stress, negatively impacting your performance and overall well-being. Knowing you have substantial contingency funds in place can significantly reduce stress and allow you to face challenges with greater confidence.

However, emergency funds alone may not be sufficient to provide all of the necessary assistance. Insurance coverage is especially useful in the event of a major health emergency, a long-term job loss, or a death in the family. It supplements any savings you already have in place, serving as an important safety net. Your insurance coverage—whether health, disability, life, or homeowner's/renter's—must be precisely tailored to your income, lifestyle, and family's unique needs. A solid financial foundation makes it much easier to care for your loved ones today and in the future. Estate planning, for example, is not only for the wealthy; it directly protects a family's future by clearly stating how assets should be distributed, outlining guardianship for minor children, and establishing any necessary trusts. Proper estate management also helps to preserve family relationships while avoiding unnecessary stress and potential disputes by establishing clear entitlements and wishes.

Pay Off Outstanding Obligations: For many, living without debt isn't just a dream—it's a powerful financial milestone. When you're not funneling your income into old obligations, you free up space to build the life you actually want. Whether it's credit cards, student loans, or a mortgage, debt eats into your ability to move forward. It forces you to spend today's earnings on yesterday's choices. And if left unmanaged, it can lead to strained credit and legal trouble. Taking back control starts with a simple but honest step: list every debt you owe, no matter how big or small. Seeing it all in one place brings the truth into focus. From there, you can create a repayment strategy that aligns with your goals—and start shifting your money toward the future instead of the past.

There are two main approaches: you can start by paying off the debts with the highest interest rates first—that's called the debt avalanche method. This strategy reduces the overall interest you pay over time by giving priority to the loans that will have the most negative financial effects. Once the largest or highest-interest debt is paid off, the payment amount is applied to the next largest or highest-interest debt, accelerating the payoff process.

Another approach is the debt snowball method, where you start by paying off your smallest debts first. This method isn't about interest rates—it's about building confidence. Each time you clear a small balance, you free up that money to tackle the next biggest one, creating a sense of momentum that keeps you going. While it may cost more in interest over time, the motivation it brings can be powerful, especially if you've struggled to stay consistent. As your debts disappear, you unlock more cash to put toward your financial goals—and with every account you close, your credit score gets a boost, opening the door to better loan terms and lower rates in the future.

Create a Tax Strategy: Strong financial habits don't just protect your money—they help you build long-term security. One smart habit is learning how to legally reduce your tax burden. For instance, some benefits your employer offers—like tuition reimbursement or monthly auto insurance—often aren't counted as taxable income. Others, like Health Savings Accounts (HSAs) and Flexible Spending Accounts

(FSAs), allow you to pay for medical costs with pre-tax dollars, meaning more of your income stays in your pocket.

If your situation allows, starting a small business—even on the side—can be a strategic move. Many legitimate business expenses, like a laptop, printer ink, advertising, or software, are deductible. These deductions lower the amount of income you're taxed on, which can translate into real savings.

But this isn't something to guess your way through. Tax rules are complex and always changing. Don't move forward with big financial changes without first getting advice from a qualified tax specialist. That fee isn't just a cost—it's a smart investment. A good professional will show you which deductions you qualify for, how to stay compliant, and how to use your current income and assets to your advantage. Their advice is tailored, not generic—and that can make a big difference in how much you keep each year.

Tips for Establishing a Solid Financial Base

A solid foundation needs to be able to endure heavy loads. With the right mindset, disciplined financial practices, and consistent effort, you can absolutely build a strong financial foundation that will last. Certain actionable tips can greatly assist you during this critical period. They include:

Establish Financial Goals with Discipline: This isn't just about wishing for a better financial future—it's about claiming it. Start by getting precise about your goals. Define what you want in the short term, in the next few years, and in the decades to come. Want to buy a home

Money Pillars

in three years? Set the number. Set the deadline. Dreaming of retiring at 60 with a solid cushion? Put it into real figures.

Discipline means showing up for those goals, especially when it's inconvenient. It means checking in, adjusting when life throws you off course, and choosing progress over impulse. It's the quiet act of putting money toward what matters—even when the tempting thing is louder.

Without clearly defined goals—ones that are specific, measurable, achievable, relevant, and time-bound—your financial direction becomes unfocused and uncertain.

Discipline brings that path into focus. It gives your money direction. It creates traction. It's not loud. But it's relentless. The kind of force that slowly—surely—changes everything.

Learn to Differentiate Between Wants and Needs: This is a fundamental concept that many people find difficult to master in practice. A need is something that is necessary for survival and basic well-being—food, shelter, utilities, and transportation. A want is something you want but can live without, such as eating out frequently, the latest smartphone, designer clothing, or an expensive vacation that you haven't saved for. Developing this discernment is essential for successful budgeting and savings. Before making a purchase, pause and honestly ask yourself: "Is this a need or a want?" If it's a want, think about if it fits into your budget or if you could use that money more wisely. This simple mental exercise, when done consistently, can have a significant impact on your spending habits and help you make financial progress. It enables you to make conscious decisions rather than reacting to impulses.

Make it a Habit to Check Your Credit Score Periodically: Your credit score is a numerical representation of your creditworthiness, or how dependable you are at repaying borrowed funds. This score is used by lenders, renters, and even some employers to assess your level of financial responsibility. A higher credit score leads to lower interest rates on loans (such as mortgages or car loans) and credit cards, potentially saving you thousands of dollars over your lifetime. Regularly checking your credit score (you are entitled to a free report from each of the three major credit bureaus every year) allows you to keep track of your financial situation. It assists you in identifying inaccuracies or fraudulent activity that may have a negative impact on your score. Your credit score is shaped by five critical elements: how reliably you pay bills, how much credit you use, the length of your credit history, recent account activity, and the variety of credit types you manage. When you understand what drives this number, you're empowered to take charge. Staying on top of these factors isn't optional—it's essential to maintaining your financial integrity.

Follow the Proper Procedures to Repay Your Obligations: This builds on the previous point about paying off debt. "Appropriate procedures" refers to a deliberate, structured approach. This isn't about throwing more money at debt whenever you feel like it. It entails determining a payoff strategy (such as the debt avalanche or snowball method), developing a detailed repayment schedule, and strictly adhering to it. It could involve consolidating high-interest debts, negotiating with creditors, or seeking professional debt counseling if your situation is dire. The goal is to gradually eliminate debt, freeing up income and increasing financial flexibility. Each debt paid off represents a significant victory, removing a burden and strengthening your financial foundation.

Create a Comprehensive Budget to Keep Track of Your Savings and Expenses: As previously discussed, budgeting is essential. A "thorough" budget is more than just keeping track of earnings and outlays. It entails categorizing every dollar and determining exactly where your money goes. This includes tracking both fixed and variable expenses. It also involves explicitly setting aside money for savings and debt repayment before spending on anything else. Your budget is a living document that you should review and adjust on a regular basis, such as weekly or monthly. It serves as your financial compass, guiding your spending and making sure you don't veer off course from your financial objectives.

Without a regularly updated budget, you're navigating your finances blindfolded. A detailed, current budget shines a light on your income, expenses, and financial habits—turning uncertainty into informed control.

Most importantly, you must fully understand this truth: you are the foundation of your financial success. While external factors and expert advice are important, your mindset, discipline, and consistent actions will ultimately determine your financial future. When planning your financial future, remember to prioritize your overall health. This includes diligently looking after your physical and mental health. Simple self-care routines such as regular exercise, mindfulness practices like yoga or meditation, and controlled breathing exercises can all help you stay in good health. A healthy mind and body provide the resilience and clarity needed to overcome financial obstacles and make sound decisions. Your well-being is inextricably linked to your financial journey; it serves as the foundation for your ability to accumulate long-term wealth and live a truly fulfilling life.

Chapter 2

Creating a Wealth-Oriented Mentality

Have you ever felt stuck? Not lazy. Not careless. Just stuck. You're doing everything they say you should—working hard, being responsible, cutting back where you can—but your bank account doesn't reflect any of it. Or maybe money slips through your fingers no matter how much you earn. More income, better budgeting—those help, sure. But that's not always the root.

Sometimes, the real shift begins in your mind.

Money Pillars

A wealth mindset begins long before your finances ever show it—it starts with how you think, not what you have.

It's about how you see money. How you think about success. How much you believe you're capable of. It's the quiet, inner shift that happens when you stop seeing limits and start seeing possibilities.

This kind of mindset doesn't happen overnight. You have to train it—like a muscle. Learn about money. Get clear on your goals. Say yes to discomfort if it moves you forward. Say no to the patterns that keep you stuck.

Building a mindset for wealth takes effort, honesty, and practice. But when you start thinking differently, you start acting differently. And eventually—your reality shifts too. Not by magic. But by clarity, commitment, and belief. One step at a time.

The True Meaning of a Wealth Mindset and Its Significance

Let's get over the technicalities. A wealth mindset isn't some magical "make it happen" dream. It's a concrete set of convictions, dispositions, and actions that put you in a position to create, develop, and yes, draw in financial prosperity. When it comes to money, your mindset is the system running everything in the background—and when that system runs on optimism and intention, it unlocks paths you didn't even know were there. Where you formerly saw barriers, you now see solutions. Where previously you only saw dead ends, you now see opportunities. It takes time to develop this mindset; you won't get it from a single lottery win or unexpected inheritance. Rather, it requires persistent work, a fundamental shift in perspective, and the conscious development of a positive attitude toward wealth and success. The catalyst for long-term financial growth is this change in viewpoint.

Beyond the financial gains, you may significantly improve your chances of attracting success and general prosperity into your life by keeping an optimistic, abundant mindset. Don't rely just on my word. In fact, a convincing 2022 study that was published in the Journal of Happiness Studies discovered that wealth development is directly influenced by good emotions. How? By actively promoting constructive habits and enhancing your cognitive abilities, which will help you think more clearly and handle problems more effectively. According to the study, positive feelings can also increase wealth by fostering positive life outcomes in a number of areas, including your job prospects, the caliber of your social relationships, and even your physical well-being. The worst part is that the authors found that people who are happier tend to save more money and have less debt. This is a strong feedback loop, not a correlation. You operate more productively and make better decisions when you're feeling happy, and your financial status reflects that. It supports the notion that your outward experience is significantly shaped by your inner world.

Consider this: what type of financial results do you think you'll produce if you're always thinking that you'll never have enough, that money is hard to get by, or that affluent people are naturally greedy? Your convictions start to come true on their own. A scarcity-minded person is concerned about getting a piece of the one pie. A wealthy mindset recognizes the possibility of discovering whole new ingredients or baking more pies. Being resourceful, upbeat, and strategic is more important than being ignorant. You understand that money is a resource and a tool that can be used to solve issues, create opportunities, and do good. When you think about money this way, you respect it, understand how it functions, and improve your ability to get and manage it. You begin to view yourself as the creator of your financial future rather than as a victim of your situation. This is about using your most potent tool—your own mind—rather than engaging in magical thinking.

Building a wealth mindset doesn't happen overnight. It's something you construct slowly—with patience, self-awareness, and a willingness to challenge the beliefs you've carried for years. Maybe you grew up in a household where money caused tension, and now you associate it with stress or fear. Or maybe past financial failures have left you feeling powerless. These experiences shape your personal "money story"—and for many people, that story is rooted in limitation.

Shifting to a wealth mindset means rewriting that story on purpose. It's a quiet but powerful shift: Instead of saying, "I can't afford this," you start asking, "How can I afford it?" Instead of thinking, "I'll always be in debt," you say, "I'm building a step-by-step plan to get out." This mindset opens the door to learning, experimenting, and taking smart risks you might have avoided before. You start behaving like someone who's capable of building wealth. You save with intention. You spend with purpose. You invest with courage.

You stop waiting for change—and start creating it. That's what a wealth mindset is about. It's not just about having money. It's about becoming the kind of person who knows how to grow and protect it.

Techniques for Developing a Wealth Mentality

Understanding what a wealth mindset means is just the beginning. True transformation happens when you shift from thinking in terms of lack to thinking in terms of possibility and abundance. This requires more than reading or reflecting—it demands a conscious effort to release what I call the "poverty mindset." These are the limiting beliefs and inherited habits that quietly sabotage your progress. They keep you from exploring new ideas, taking smart risks, or believing you're even capable of achieving financial freedom. You might not even realize you've built invisible walls around your own potential.

Breaking through those walls is the real work. And it starts with intentional action. Here are three practical ways to begin rewiring your mind for lasting wealth:

Attend Abundance Events (Selectively): If you are truly prepared to transform your life and start down a path of wealth and prosperity, look for and go to what some refer to as "abundance events." These aren't just happy-making events; the best ones, which are frequently hosted by seasoned financial experts or successful business owners, help you understand why the world needs you to be wealthy. They contradict the stories you tell yourself. The goal of these activities is to assist you in recognizing and proactively overcoming the ingrained, constricting mindsets that have prevented you from moving forward. You'll be inspired to develop several sources of wealth and start enjoying the financial life you've always dreamed of when you break down those internal obstacles. But exercise discernment. Seek out events with a proven track record, specific learning goals, and testimonies that discuss practical tactics rather than only inspirational platitudes. You're not looking for clichés; you're looking for real insights. Making connections with others who have successfully walked the path to wealth and gleaning their practical ideas is where the true value lies. This is about targeted inspiration and smart learning, not mindless faith.

Money Pillars

Consider it this way: if you want to become a master carpenter, you don't simply study tools; you also attend seminars, watch masters in action, pick up their methods, and develop a new perspective on wood. At its best, an abundance event provides a comparable level of immersion into the psychology and realities of wealth generation. It presents you with fresh perspectives on money, risk, opportunity, and individual accountability. It enables you to see that wealth is not a limited pie in which your gain is someone else's loss. Rather, it teaches you how to recognize and contribute to the development of new values, increasing the share of wealth for all. You often walk away with clearer eyes—suddenly aware of blind spots you hadn't seen before, reconnected to a sense of purpose, and equipped with concrete steps forward. It all begins with changing your inner dialogue—because when your self-talk shifts, your actions follow.

Surround Yourself with Positive and Successful People: If you want to develop a wealthy mindset, you must be intentional about the company you keep. That means surrounding yourself with people who are actively striving for growth, success, and a life filled with purpose. This isn't always easy. Sometimes, it requires cutting ties or creating distance from those who drain your energy—people who constantly complain about money, mock ambition, or treat success with jealousy or doubt. That kind of scarcity thinking is contagious. Whether you notice it or not, the beliefs, habits, and emotional tone of the people closest to you will eventually rub off on you.

But the reverse is also true—when you spend time with driven, financially healthy, and genuinely optimistic people, you gain more than inspiration. You gain insight. You see how they make decisions, how they recover from losses, how they stay focused. These relationships open doors to mentorship, collaboration, and learning through example. You begin to adopt their discipline, their habits, their mindset—not through imitation, but through alignment.

This is about more than networking. It's about choosing influences that stretch you, challenge you, and remind you of what's possible. Those closest to you gradually mold how you think, act, and dream—until their patterns become part of your own without you even noticing.

So ask yourself: are they lifting you toward your highest financial self—or anchoring you to the same old limitations?

Set Clear, Measurable Goals: Changing your perspective is only one aspect of cultivating a wealth mindset. To believe and do nothing is to wish. The next step is to set specific, measurable goals that will help you stay motivated and start the process of accumulating wealth. It takes continuous, constructive, and intentional financial actions, such as careful planning, disciplined saving, and strategic investing, to build wealth. Every single step, no matter how tiny, helps you build vital momentum and gets you closer to your financial goals. To create objectives that actually produce outcomes, use these guidelines:

1. Be Clear About Your Goal: One of the biggest reasons people miss their financial targets is because their goals remain vague and undefined. Absolute clarity is the foundation of every effective financial plan—without it, progress is just guesswork.

You have to be crystal clear about your financial targets—maybe it's pulling in an extra $2,000 each month through a freelance project, directing funds into well-defined investments, or setting up a routine where 15% to 20% of your income is automatically saved without second thought.

A goal like "I'll grow my net worth by $50,000 over the next year" gives you direction and urgency. On the other hand, saying "I want more money" leaves you spinning your wheels. You have to be exact. Put your target in sharp focus.

2. Establish Quantifiable Goals: Your financial targets should be rooted in real, trackable numbers—not vague hopes. This means defining targets you can track and quantify—like setting a clear revenue benchmark for a skill you're monetizing or a monthly sales figure for a business initiative. Specific numbers create structure and accountability. For example: "By December 31st, I'll be generating an extra $5,000 a month from freelance work and will have eliminated $10,000 in credit card debt." Or, "I'll build a $7,500 emergency fund by October 1st by automating $625 monthly transfers into a separate savings account." If it can't be measured, it can't be managed—or improved.

3. Establish Long-term and Short-term Goals: The strategic separation of long-term and short-term objectives offers a very clear, doable route to financial security, just like quantifiable goals do. Long-term goals could be starting a profitable business that brings in passive income, purchasing a primary dwelling or an investment property, or setting up a complete retirement savings plan. These are your final financial landmarks and your destination points. On the other hand, short-term objectives are the vital first steps toward those longer-term objectives. These could include setting up that first emergency fund, paying off a particular high-interest loan, putting money aside for a course that will help you develop your skills, or making your first small investment. Both the final destination and the first measures you take to get there need to be crystal clear in your mind. The short-term goals feed into the long-term ones, creating a powerful sense of momentum and achievement.

4. Hold Yourself Accountable: Wealth accountability means owning your financial decisions with intention and regularly checking in—sometimes relentlessly—on your goals and habits. It's about taking full responsibility for your money choices and the outcomes they lead to. But it's not a solo mission. One of the smartest moves you can make is inviting someone you trust—whether a financially savvy friend or a seasoned mentor—to help keep you in check. A good accountability partner won't just celebrate your wins; they'll question poor spending habits, challenge your thinking with care, and remind you of your long-term vision when your own drive runs low. This isn't about guilt or pressure. It's about creating a system of encouragement and alignment to help you stay the course.

Strategic Risk-Taking: Building real wealth almost always requires stepping beyond your comfort zone and embracing well-calculated

Money Pillars

risks. Sticking only to "safe" financial moves may feel secure, but over time, it can limit your growth. The most rewarding investments—whether financial, educational, or entrepreneurial—tend to involve some level of uncertainty. But this doesn't mean reckless gambling or risking everything when you're already financially stretched. Calculated risks are grounded in research, preparation, and a clear understanding of what's at stake. You weigh the upside, assess the downside, and take protective steps. Maybe it's launching a side business after analyzing the market, investing in a stock after studying its track record, or enrolling in a program to increase your long-term income potential. These aren't impulsive moves—they're intentional decisions based on logic, not fear. Wealth grows where courage meets clarity.

Establishing Objectives, Practicing Patience, and Fostering Perseverance

It's crucial to practice patience as you start this significant shift toward new financial behaviors and cognitive patterns. This is a marathon, not a race. Setting goals with diligence, committing to ongoing financial education, taking strategic risks, courage, and deliberately surrounding yourself with successful, inspirational people are the first steps in developing a true wealth mindset. Think about this: if you choose your "abundance" or wealth retreat carefully, it may also be a huge boost, assisting you in bringing your financial objectives and your inner compass into alignment. It can provide you with a concentrated dose of the necessary mental adjustments and useful techniques. Whatever route you decide to pursue to build financial riches, know this: every conscious move you take to achieve your objectives will strongly reinforce your conviction that you are deserving of wealth. It reaffirms that prosperity is attainable for those who put in the effort and isn't reserved for a chosen few. Your consistent efforts, no matter how minor, create an indisputable momentum. They show you that you are capable, worthy, and actively building the financial life you have always desired. Your perseverance, driven by a positive, wealth-oriented mindset, will ultimately get you through the journey's bumps and difficulties.

Chapter 3

Investment Strategies

An investment strategy is your financial compass—it guides your decisions and keeps you steady through market uncertainty. At first, the investing world can feel overwhelming, like stepping into deep, unfamiliar waters. But you don't need to be an expert to find your footing. With proven strategies and a clear plan, you can simplify the journey. Whether you're aiming for long-term wealth, steady passive income, or financial independence, the right approach aligns your actions with your goals. Investing isn't reserved for the elite—it's for anyone willing to learn, commit, and move with intention.

Laying the Groundwork: Key Investment Concepts for Beginners

A well-crafted investment strategy serves a dual purpose: it helps manage risk while positioning you for meaningful returns. It's a careful balance—one you must acknowledge from the start. Market-based assets like stocks and bonds can fluctuate, and short-term losses are part of the journey. It's not a setback—it's part of how long-term wealth is built. Investing isn't about chasing quick wins or beating the system. That mindset often leads to reckless decisions. Instead, approach investing with grounded expectations. You're building lasting wealth—not buying a winning ticket. Real success comes with time, patience, and a plan you can stick with.

Let's look at five popular investment approaches geared toward novices. We'll look at their specific advantages as well as the risks they pose. Before you invest your hard-earned money, you must consider both sides of the equation.

Buy and Hold: The Power of Patience
Buy-and-hold investing remains one of the most reliable paths to building wealth over time. At its core, this approach is simple: you purchase an asset and commit to keeping it for the long haul—often with no set intention to sell. While the option to exit always exists, the mindset here is patience, not quick profits. Ideally, you're holding onto that investment for at least three to five years, if not decades. The principle behind this strategy is straightforward—despite temporary market dips or volatility, strong,

well-chosen assets typically increase in value over time. It's a long game grounded in consistency and trust in long-term growth.

Advantages:

The buy-and-hold strategy fundamentally switches your attention to the long run. It forces you to think as a business owner rather than a speculative trader. This intrinsic long-term concentration lets you escape the costly traps of active trading, which, ironically, frequently depletes the gains of most individual investors. Constant buying and selling increases transaction expenses and, more importantly, tempts you to respond emotionally to every market dip or spike. Your buy-and-hold investing success is directly related to the long-term performance and growth of the underlying firm or asset in which you have invested. This strategy positions you to eventually discover and capitalize on the stock market's biggest winners, potentially earning returns hundreds of times your initial investment. You are planting a tree and allowing it to develop, rather than harvesting seedlings on a daily basis. Another important advantage of this technique arises if you are truly committed to never selling, or at least holding for decades. Capital gains taxes are successfully postponed and sometimes avoided entirely. These taxes, charged on the profit you generate when selling an investment, can significantly reduce your overall returns. Simply holding makes more of your money work for you. Furthermore, unlike active traders, long-term buy-and-hold strategies do not require you to be continually riveted to market screens. This frees up your time and mental energy, allowing you to concentrate on your profession, family, and interests while actually enjoying your life, rather than being constantly linked to market changes. You set it up, tend it, and let time do the heavy labor.

Risks:

To truly succeed with the buy-and-hold strategy, you must have a strong will. You must absolutely resist the temptation to sell when the market eventually becomes tumultuous. There will be major declines—market corrections of at least 10% or bear markets of at least 20%, 30%, or even 50%. Individual stocks, in particular, can experience even steeper declines. Having your portfolio worth cut in half, even briefly, can be terrifying. This is a gut check. Selling during these downturns locks in your losses and keeps you from profiting from the inevitable comeback. It's much harder to do this than to say it. The emotional discipline necessary is typically the most difficult challenge for beginning investors. You need to believe in the market's long-term trajectory and remember why you invested in the first place. You're buying excellent firms, and great companies typically recover.

Invest in Index Funds

Invest in index funds to own the entire market rather than just a portion of it.

This technique simplifies investing by emphasizing a concept rather than individual stock selection. It's all about finding an appealing stock index and then buying an index fund that matches it. Popular stock market indices include the Standard & Poor's 500 (S&P 500), which measures 500 of the largest publicly traded firms in the United States, and the Nasdaq

Composite, which is heavily weighted in technology equities. Each of these indexes offers a diverse variety of the market's best shares, resulting in a highly diversified portfolio of assets, even if this index fund is your only investment. Instead of trying to outsmart the market by picking individual stocks—which even experienced investors rarely do consistently—you buy the entire market through a fund and benefit from its broad, long-term growth.

Advantages:

Buying an index fund is a very simple technique that routinely provides great long-term returns, especially when combined with the aforementioned buy-and-hold mentality. Your return will be directly proportional to the weighted average performance of the assets contained within the index. Crucially, a varied portfolio minimizes risk compared to owning only a few specific equities. If one firm in the index performs poorly, its impact on your overall return is negligible because it is outweighed by hundreds of other companies. Moreover, by eliminating the need to constantly research, analyze, and handpick individual stocks, this strategy demands far less effort on your part. Your investments quietly grow in the background while you focus your energy on work, family, or passions that matter to you. It's a smart, truly passive approach to building long-term wealth.

Risks:
While there are always risks associated with investing in the stock market, maintaining a varied portfolio of equities, such as through an

index fund, is typically seen as a far safer option than focusing your money in a few specific firms. However, if you truly want to reach the market's historical long-term gains—which for the S&P 500 have averaged over 10% per year for several decades—you must stay invested even throughout the inevitable bad times. You cannot panic and sell when the market falls. If you do, you forfeit the recovery. Furthermore, because you are acquiring a portfolio of hundreds or thousands of companies, you will earn the average market return rather than the potentially astronomical returns (or devastating losses) associated with selecting only the most popular or fastest-growing individual stocks. However, and this is essential, most investors, including professionals with substantial resources, regularly struggle to exceed these broad market averages over time. So, while you may not get the greatest stock, you are almost guaranteed to receive the average market return, which has historically been pretty high.

Index and a Few: Combining Stability with Selectivity

The "index and a few" strategy builds on the simplicity of index fund investing but adds a personal touch for those who want a bit more control or excitement in their portfolio. You start by anchoring most of your investment—say, 85–95%—in a diversified index fund, ensuring broad market exposure and lower risk. Then, with the remaining portion, you handpick a few individual stocks you strongly believe in. Maybe it's a tech giant you admire for its innovation or a sustainable company aligned with your values. This approach lets you enjoy the steady reliability of index investing while still allowing room for personal conviction plays—without taking on the full risk of stock-picking.

Advantages:

This hybrid strategy thoughtfully merges the strengths of index investing with the excitement and growth potential of individual stock picking. You maintain the stability and ease of a broad, diversified foundation—minimizing risk and effort—while giving yourself space to explore. Those handpicked stocks aren't just for potential gains; they're also a learning tool. By allocating a small slice of your portfolio to companies you've researched and believe in, you build confidence and skill as an investor. If one doesn't work out, your core holdings keep you steady. It's like training wheels for stock selection—smart, strategic, and designed to grow with you.

Risks:

As long as these individual, selected positions account for a small portion of your entire portfolio (preferably no more than 10-20%), the risks are very similar to those inherent in pure index investing. You will still receive roughly the market's average return until your few individual picks turn out to be either incredibly outstanding or catastrophically terrible. However, there is one important caveat: if you want to invest in certain companies, you must first devote significant time and effort to learning how to thoroughly study them. This includes knowing their business concepts, financial health, competitive landscape, and management team. Without adequate study and analysis, you are only speculating, not investing. If you don't do your study, your portfolio's particular stock component may suffer a loss for which you will be solely responsible. This method requires discipline in both allocation and research.

Income Investing: Be Paid to Own Assets

Income investing focuses on owning investments that routinely generate cash payments. These payments are often made in the form of cash dividends from stocks or regular interest payments from bonds. This strategy has the direct benefit of delivering a portion of your total return in the form of hard cash, which you can then spend on whatever you want, or, more strategically, reinvest those proceeds in other income-producing stocks or bonds. If you own high-quality dividend stocks, you may benefit from both consistent cash income and potential capital gains if the stock price rises over time.

Advantages:

Even as a beginner, you may simply apply an income-investing strategy by investing in income-focused index funds or Exchange Traded Funds (ETFs) that specialize in dividend stocks or bonds. This strategy successfully eliminates the need for you to select particular stocks and bonds, which necessitate extensive investigation. Income investments are less volatile in value than high-growth stocks, providing a higher level of stability. You might also expect to receive consistent cash income from your investments, which can be a reassuring and reliable source of finances. Furthermore, high-quality dividend equities, which are frequently issued by mature, financially sound corporations, typically grow in dividend payouts over time. This means that the amount of cash income you receive increases without any additional effort from you, making dividend investing one of the most effective and truly passive income strategies available. Imagine earning more money from your investments year after year simply because the company in which you own a stake continues to develop and share its profits.

Risks:

While income stocks are often less volatile and risky than many high-growth stocks, they are nonetheless equities, which means that their prices might fall dramatically during market downturns or if the underlying company confronts serious issues. If you invest in individual income stocks, there is always the danger that the company could lower or abolish its dividend, leaving you with no payout and possibly a financial loss if the stock price falls as a result. Bond rates, especially during times of low interest rates, are not always appealing. They can be so low that they fail to cover the rate of inflation, ultimately reducing investors' purchasing power over time. Furthermore, and this is a key tax concern, if you keep bonds and dividend stocks in a normal, taxable brokerage account, you will often be obliged to pay income taxes on those dividend and interest payments each year. To defer or reduce these taxes, you may want to consider holding these income-producing assets in a retirement account, such as a 401(k) or an IRA (Individual Retirement Account), where they can grow tax-deferred or even tax-free (a Roth IRA).

Dollar-Cost Averaging: Smoothing the Ride

Dollar-cost averaging removes emotion from the equation. Instead of stressing about whether the market is too high or too low, you build a habit—investing on schedule, like clockwork. Some months, your $500 buys fewer shares when prices are high. Other months, it buys more when prices dip. Over time, this smooths out the impact of market volatility and often results in a lower average cost per share. It's consistent. Predictable. Stress-free. And most importantly, it helps you stay invested—one of the most powerful habits for long-term wealth.

Advantages:

Spreading out your buy points through dollar-cost averaging considerably reduces the danger of "timing the market." Timing the market refers to the extremely tough, virtually impossible task of investing all of your money at the absolute lowest point and selling at the absolute highest point. Most individual investors, and even most pros, routinely fail at this. Dollar-cost averaging ensures that you do not "overpay" by pouring big sums of money into the market just before a significant drop. When prices rise, your set dollar amount buys fewer shares; when prices fall, it buys more. This gradually averages out your purchasing price. Furthermore, dollar-cost averaging is an extremely successful method for developing a consistent, disciplined investment routine. Emotion is removed from the equation. Simply automate the procedure. If you stick to this method over time, you will almost certainly build a considerably larger and more valuable investment portfolio. Consistency, not precise timing, is essential here.

Risks:

While the disciplined, consistent strategy of dollar-cost averaging completely stops you from going "all-in" at the worst possible time (just before a market crash), it also means you won't go "all-in" when you potentially should. As a result, you are unlikely to get the absolute maximum return on your investment, as opposed to a hypothetical situation in which you invested a large lump sum at the market's lowest point. However, this is a modest theoretical disadvantage when compared to the enormous practical advantage of preventing catastrophic timing errors.

The real beauty of this approach lies in its simplicity. You're not trying to guess the next market bottom or top. You're just showing up—month after month—letting time and discipline do the heavy lifting..And over the years, that quiet consistency adds up. You may never brag about buying at the lowest price, but you also won't suffer the regret of jumping in too high and bailing out too low. For most people, especially beginners, this steady rhythm is the difference between building real wealth and burning out chasing perfection.

Bottom Line: Your Investing Journey Begins Now

The world of investment may appear huge and convoluted. New investors frequently believe they must grasp every single element before they can even begin. But, good news: you don't. Beginners may make investing shockingly simple by taking a few basic actions and, most importantly, allowing time and the market's long-term trends to do the hard work for them. You don't have to be a stock selection expert.

Money Pillars

Investing can be one of the most beneficial financial decisions you ever make for yourself. It is the primary driver of long-term wealth generation. However, as we have discussed, the process can be difficult, particularly emotionally. Simplify things for yourself: choose one or two fundamental investment strategies that are appropriate for your risk tolerance and financial goals, and then adhere to them with unshakable dedication. As you get more experience and a better grasp of how investing works, you might start to consider diversifying your techniques and broadening your investment options. The key is to begin now, start simply, and maintain consistency.

Chapter 4

Building Wealth Using Real Estate

The Foundation: Understanding Real Estate as an Asset

Many people aspire to own property, whether it's their first house or an investment. Beyond the emotional connection, real estate is an effective tool for wealth accumulation. It's more than just having a place to live; it's about obtaining an asset that will appreciate in value, provide income, and bring major financial benefits over time. Forget the get-rich-quick scams you've seen advertised. Real estate wealth development is often a long-term endeavor that takes patience, research, and a thorough understanding of the underlying principles.

Consider this: when you buy stock, you own a small portion of the corporation. When you buy real estate, you acquire a tangible item - a plot of land or a structure - that people will constantly require for housing, trade, or industry. This inherent need ensures stability that other investments may lack. While the stock market can be volatile, with sharp fluctuations based on news cycles or investor mood, real estate typically moves at a slower pace. This is not to say that it is immune to downturns; rather, its cycles are longer and more predictable, allowing for smart entry and exit opportunities.

Think of appreciation as the quiet power behind real estate wealth—the rise in a property's value simply because time passes and the world around it changes. You don't always see it happening, but it builds beneath the surface. Maybe the neighborhood gets a new train line. Maybe a tech company sets up shop a few blocks away. Maybe more families move in, looking for good schools. These shifts drive up demand. That same $200,000 house you bought a few years ago? It could be worth $300,000 without you lifting more than a paintbrush. That $100,000 difference—that's appreciation working for you. But it's not guaranteed. If jobs leave town, or the area stops developing, values can stagnate or drop. That's why buying the house is only half the battle. The bigger move is picking the right place. Pay attention to future zoning plans, school ratings, commute routes, and neighborhood energy. Talk to locals. Walk the streets at different times. Don't just chase a deal—learn the story of the area. That's where appreciation begins.

Another significant advantage of real estate is income generating, especially with investment buildings. This is mostly derived from rent. When you own a rental property, renters pay you monthly, which covers your mortgage, property taxes, insurance, and maintenance expenses. After these expenses, the residual funds are your cash flow. The idea is to have positive cash flow, which implies that the property puts money in your pocket every month, even before you factor in appreciation. Let's say you acquire a duplex. You rent out one unit and live in the other. The rent you get from your tenant could greatly offset your mortgage payment, lowering your own housing costs and helping you to build equity more quickly. Alternatively, you may buy a single-family home and rent it out altogether. The trick here is to carefully balance possible rental income with all of your expenses, including vacancy rates. Many rookie investors overestimate revenue while underestimating expenses, resulting in negative cash flow. That is a circumstance in which the property becomes a financial drain rather than a wealth producer. You'll need to look into local rental rates, understand normal operating costs in the area, and include a buffer in your projections for unforeseen repairs or times of vacancy.

Then there is leverage. This is probably the most compelling feature of real estate investing for many people. The use of borrowed money, typically obtained through a mortgage, to take control of a bigger asset is known as leverage. You put down a modest fraction of the buying price, and the bank covers the remainder. For example, if you buy a $300,000 home with a 20% down payment, you have only spent $60,000 of your own money. If that property appreciates by 5% per year, it is currently worth $315,000. Thanks to the leverage, your initial $60,000 investment has increased by $15,000 (a 25% return on your invested capital, ignoring costs). Without leverage, you'd need the entire $300,000 to purchase the property altogether, and a 5% appreciation would result in a 5% return on your investment. Leverage boosts your profits, but it also increases your risk. If the value of your house falls, your equity will erode even faster. Understanding your debt-to-income ratio, having a consistent income, and preserving an emergency fund to make mortgage payments in the event of unanticipated circumstances are all examples of responsible leverage. Do not overextend yourself.

Finally, consider the tax advantages. Mortgage interest, property taxes, insurance, and depreciation are common expenses that property owners can deduct. Depreciation is especially interesting since it is a non-cash expense that reduces your taxable income even when the property's value increases. The IRS essentially recognizes that buildings don't last forever—they wear down over time. While we won't go into the specifics of tax law here (always consult a certified tax professional), realizing that these benefits exist can have a major impact on your overall return on investment. This is one more reason real estate remains such a powerful wealth-building tool over time. These tax breaks aren't some secret—Congress put them there on purpose to make property investment more attractive.

Strategic Acquisitions: Buying Smart for Long-Term Gain

Purchasing real estate is a significant financial choice, whether for investment or personal use. It's not just about scoring a bargain or picking a home that looks great. The real goal is to make a smart, strategic purchase that fits your financial goals and builds long-term value. That means understanding the market, doing thorough research, and approaching every offer with clarity and intention. A successful real estate investment cannot be discovered by chance; it must be built brick by brick via wise decisions. Start by learning about your local market. This goes beyond just knowing the average worth of a home. Understand the supply and demand for homes in your chosen location. Is there more buying than selling, indicating a seller's market with rising prices? Or is it a buyer's market with plenty of inventory, giving you more bargaining power? Analyze the last six to twelve months' worth of comparable property sales data. How quickly do homes sell? Are they selling above, at, or below the asking price? These indicators provide an accurate view of the market's health and trajectory.

Pay attention to the area's economic drivers, which include new enterprises, job growth, infrastructure developments, and demographic shifts. When a city invests in its downtown or attracts significant firms, it frequently indicates future property value development. In contrast, an area experiencing job losses or population decline may see stagnant or falling property values. Don't just believe what a real estate agent tells you; conduct your own research using internet property portals, local government planning websites, and economic development reports. You're establishing your own knowledge base, which will allow you to make smarter judgments.

Once you've chosen a suitable region, the following step is to conduct due diligence on individual homes. Now is the time to get down to business and start working on the details. For an investment home, you look at more than just the curb appeal; you also consider the figures. What is the possible rental income? Examine the rental prices of comparable homes in the neighborhood. Verify a landlord's word rather than just taking it at its value. What are the operational expenses? This covers property

Money Pillars

taxes, insurance, upkeep, utilities (if you are responsible for them), and prospective vacancy rates. Get insurance estimates, look at property tax records, and create a realistic budget for repairs and maintenance.

A decent rule of thumb for maintenance is to budget 1-2% of the property's worth each year, though this can vary. This amounts to $2,000-$4,000 each year for a $200,000 home. You would be astonished at how quickly little fixes add up. Don't forget to get a home inspection on any property you're serious about. This is an essential investment, not an optional one. A professional inspector will detect potential concerns such as a leaking roof, bad wiring, or plumbing difficulties, which might cost you tens of thousands of dollars in the long run. Knowing about these difficulties ahead of time provides you leverage when negotiating the price or requesting that the seller make repairs. It's far better to walk away from a bargain than to purchase a money hole.

Before you begin seriously looking into finance, you must first get pre-approved for a mortgage. This tells you just how much you can spend and indicates to vendors that you are a genuine buyer. Search for the best mortgage rates and terms. Even a half percentage point change in your interest rate can save you thousands of dollars over the course of the loan. Choose the mortgage that best fits your risk tolerance and financial circumstances by being aware of the several mortgage kinds (fixed-rate and adjustable-rate). A fixed-rate mortgage provides regular payments, but an adjustable-rate mortgage may start lower but fluctuate, creating anxiety. Don't just accept the first offer from your bank; speak with many lenders, including credit unions and mortgage brokers. They frequently have access to a broader choice of products and can obtain a more competitive price.

Making an offer takes a deliberate strategy. Your offer price should be determined by your market research and the condition of the property, rather than your emotional attachment. Be prepared to negotiate. Few offers are accepted at the full asking price, particularly in a buyer's market. Your offer should include conditions such as a satisfactory home inspection, an appraisal that matches the purchase price, and clear financing approval. These contingencies will safeguard you if anything unexpected happens. For example, if the appraisal is lower than your offer, the bank will not lend you as much, and you will be required to make up the difference or renegotiate the price. Without an assessment contingency, you may be stuck. Remember that it is acceptable to walk away if the numbers do not work or if the inspection shows too many issues. There will always be additional properties. Don't let emotion or the fear of missing out pressure you into making a terrible transaction. In the real estate industry, patience is a virtue.

Finally, evaluate your exit strategy even before making a purchase. What are your plans for eventually selling the property or realizing your gains? Is it a primary residence that you plan to eventually rent out, a short-term flip, or a long-term rental? Being aware of your exit strategy enables you to make better choices in advance. You want consistent cash flow and slow appreciation if it's a rental. You have to be sure that you can increase value while selling quickly if you're flipping. Your purchase procedure will become clearer if you start with the end in mind. Strategic acquisitions provide the groundwork for long-term wealth creation in real estate. They eliminate most of the guessing and replace it with measured, informed decisions.

Sustaining Growth: Management, Maintenance, and Maximum Returns

Purchasing a property is only the beginning. Maintaining real estate growth requires active management, meticulous maintenance, and a constant search for ways to enhance returns. This is not a passive investment that you can buy and forget about. To truly generate wealth, you must treat your property as a small business, ensuring that it operates smoothly and productively.

For rental homes, competent property management is essential. You have two options: hire an experienced property manager or do it yourself. Although self-management saves you management costs (about 8–12% of gross rents) and gives you direct control, it takes time and work.

You're in charge of locating and screening tenants, collecting rent, resolving maintenance requests, dealing with crises, and following tenant rules. This might be a full-time job, particularly if you own several houses. If you're considering self-management, be honest about your time commitment and level of comfort with these obligations. You'll need a strong lease agreement, a rent collection system, and reputable repair contractors. Understanding local landlord-tenant regulations is crucial; a misstep can result in significant legal complications.

Hiring a property manager alleviates these tasks. They are in charge of everything from promoting vacant properties and screening tenants to collecting rent and coordinating upkeep. While they charge a fee, a professional manager can help you save money in the long term by rapidly finding reliable tenants, collecting rent on time, and avoiding costly legal issues. They frequently have established contacts with contractors, which may allow them to offer you better repair costs. A property manager might be an excellent investment for out-of-state investors or those with limited time. When selecting a manager, seek for someone with an established track record, positive references, and clear communication skills. Inquire about the tenant screening process, how they manage evictions, and their cost structure. Don't choose the cheapest option; quality management has a direct impact on your bottom line.

Maintenance is another important part of sustaining growth. A property that is kept up maintains its value and draws in desired renters. Deferred maintenance, on the other hand, can easily escalate into larger, more expensive problems and lower the value of your house. Consider it a means of protecting your resources. Create a preventative maintenance routine that includes frequent HVAC inspections, gutter cleaning, landscaping, and pest treatment. Take care of small issues as soon as you can to keep them from growing into bigger ones. A leaking faucet is more than simply an irritation; if ignored, it can cause water damage and mold. Create a reserve fund expressly for unexpected repairs. Things break, roofs leak, and appliances become worn out. Being prepared for these unavoidable expenses keeps them from disrupting your financial flow or putting you in debt. It's far preferable to replace an outdated water heater in advance than to cope with a burst pipe in the middle of the night.

Beyond routine maintenance, consider value-added enhancements to maximize your profits. These are strategic improvements or upgrades that boost the property's value and rental income. For example, updating a kitchen or bathroom in a rental property may justify a higher rent. Building a deck or completing a basement can increase a home's resale value. Not all changes provide the same return on investment, so investigate what is most wanted in your market. A fresh coat of paint and new flooring are generally inexpensive methods to remodel a home and appeal to potential tenants or buyers. Before starting a large remodeling, consider the possible return. Will the increased rent or sale price cover the cost of the renovations? Avoid over-improving the area; you don't want to have the prettiest house on the block if you won't be able to repay your investment.

Finally, strategic refinancing can help sustain expansion. If interest rates fall dramatically, refinancing your mortgage may result in lower monthly payments, freeing up cash flow. If your property has appreciated significantly, you may be eligible to do a cash-out refinance, which allows you to withdraw some of your equity to invest in another property or pursue other financial goals. This is a type of leverage that demands careful evaluation. You're taking on extra debt, so make sure your financial situation is stable enough to handle it. Always consider the costs of refinancing (origination, appraisal, and other fees) against the potential advantages. It is not always the best option, but it is a tool in your armory.

Using real estate to build wealth is a process rather than a final goal. It takes regular effort, sound decisions, and a dedication to safeguarding and increasing your wealth. By actively managing your properties, keeping up with upkeep, and proactively looking for methods to enhance value, you can maximize your returns and secure your financial future. It's about being proactive, rather than reactive, in all aspects of your real estate assets.

Chapter 5

Debt Management

If you're struggling with unsecured debt, debt management may be able to assist you keep up with your payments. You can manage your debt in a variety of ways, including the debt snowball method and engaging with a credit counseling agency. When you do, you'll be able to create a debt management strategy that is appropriate for your budget and financial situation.

Credit cards make it easier to pay for large purchases or bills, but managing debt and making timely payments is not always that easy. Most Americans own at least one credit card, with an average balance of slightly more than $6,500 as of 2023. Debt management is one of various options for helping you manage debt that has gotten out of control.

What is Debt Management?

Debt management is the process of bringing your debt under control through financial planning and budgeting. The goal of a debt management strategy is to lower your current debt and eventually eliminate it.

You can create a debt management plan for yourself or seek credit counseling. Both options have advantages and disadvantages. The simplest method is to devise a strategy on your own, however having an outside partner provide negotiation support, accountability, or both.

How Does Debt Management Work?

Debt management methods focus on unsecured debts like credit cards and personal loans. Debt management usually takes one of three forms.

DIY Debt Management

The first option is to handle your debts on your own. With this method, you create a budget for yourself that allows you to meet your obligations while remaining financially stable. The debt snowball and debt avalanche are the two most common DIY debt management approaches.

Who is this better for? If you struggle with overspending but can afford to make monthly debt payments by being more disciplined, this method may be right for you.

The main benefit is that you may protect your credit rating by making on-time monthly payments and paying in whole. You can also create a realistic plan with milestones and a debt-payoff date to stay motivated throughout the repayment process.

The most significant disadvantage is that you will not have access to assistance from a professional who may have more effective strategies for getting out of debt faster. Furthermore, creditors might not be willing to compromise.

Budget and repayment calculators, together with financial management tools, will help you stay on track. If necessary, you may negotiate with your creditors to lower your monthly payments or interest rates. Once the debt is under control, you can choose to keep or close the account.

Debt Management With a Credit Counsellor

The second method of debt management is credit counseling. You can find a credit counselor in your area by searching the National Foundation of Credit Counselors. Credit counselors might be nonprofit or for-profit. Before enrolling in a credit counseling programme, research reviews and understand any associated expenses.

A credit counselor can help you create a repayment schedule and, if necessary, negotiate a debt management plan (DMP) with your creditors. It often lasts three to five years and includes perks like lower interest rates, lower monthly payments, or fee waivers to help you pay off debt faster. Depending on your situation, the creditor may terminate your accounts as each loan is paid off to avoid acquiring new debt.

This is ideal for people who seek professional help with their finances and credit score.

The most major advantage is that debt management plans are usually less expensive than paying creditors directly. If the talks are successful, you will receive a fixed monthly payment as well as a debt repayment schedule. The collection calls will terminate. Furthermore, the impact on your credit score would be less pronounced than if you settled the debts for less than you owed.

The main downside is that you may be unable to utilize your credit accounts during the DMP. Furthermore, you will relinquish authority over your commitments to the counseling service. Typically, the agency accepts a single monthly payment, which may include a monthly fee, and distributes it to your creditors.

Debt Relief Company

You can also hire a debt relief agency to assist you in resolving your outstanding unsecured bills. Debt reduction companies work with creditors and lenders to reach settlements for less than you owe.

When you sign up, you commit to making monthly payments to the debt relief agency. Your payments are stored in an account that only you have access to. In the meantime, many debt relief firms advise you to cease paying creditors and lenders in order to expedite the negotiation process.

You will be notified once a resolution has been reached. If you approve, the payment will be made with funds from the account into which you have been paying. The debt settlement company will also deduct a settlement fee from the same account.

Who is this best for? Debt relief may be beneficial for persons who are drowning in unsecured debt, have attempted to settle debt on their own without success, and do not want to declare bankruptcy.

The most major advantage is that you might be able to lower your monthly debt payments. Accepting settlement offers may allow you to pay off your debts faster and keep more money in your pocket.

The most important disadvantages are that creditors and lenders are not obligated to accept settlement proposals, which could land you in court, and that settling your debts for less than the full amount outstanding will almost likely hurt your credit score. Furthermore, if the forgiven amount exceeds $600, you may have to pay federal income taxes.

How Might Debt Management Help?

Find a licensed non profit debt management company. Although not all countries need debt management service providers to be licensed, it is generally a good idea to inquire. A debt management firm's participation in a professional organization, such as the Financial Counseling Group of America or the National Foundation of Credit Counselors, is also advantageous.

Cambridge Credit Counseling claims to have lowered monthly credit card payments by an average of 25%. The company also claims to have decreased the average credit card interest rate from 22% to 8%. It also advertises a 48-month average loan repayment period.

Is Debt Management Suitable for You?

Debt management can be an effective technique for debt relief, but it is not quick. Debt management does not include secured debts such as mortgages or vehicle loans. However, it may be worth looking into if you:

- Have many high-interest, unsecured debts, such as credit cards.

- Are approaching or at the maximum credit limit for each account.

- Have a steady income to cover your bills.

- Don't expect to open a new credit account during your DMP.

- Instead of negotiating your DMP on your own, consider hiring an agency or firm.

- Have addressed dangerous financial behaviors such as overspending.

Does Debt Management Impact Your Credit Score?

While debt management might help you get debt under control, it can have a negative impact on your credit score.

Hard Questions

A hard inquiry may occur at several occasions during debt management. For example, if you try to negotiate a lower interest rate, you may face a hard inquiry. Hard inquiries remain on your credit report for two years and can affect your credit score for one year.

However, this is a temporary effect that can be easily mitigated by other circumstances. For example, lowering your interest rate and consistently paying your monthly bill can improve your payment history, which accounts for 35% of your credit score.

Missed Payments

While making consistent payments improves your payment history, missing payments will dramatically lower your credit score. If you or your credit counselor use the method of withholding payment from your creditors in order to obtain a lower interest rate, your credit score will suffer.

Credit Utilization

Another important aspect in determining the health of your credit score is credit use. It accounts for 30% of your credit score and is based on how much debt you have relative to your available credit. The ideal credit utilization is between 10% and 30%. This means your debt should not exceed 30% of your available credit across all accounts.

Consolidating your debt into a single installment will help you pay it off faster. However, closing accounts that you consolidate may boost your credit utilization ratio. DMPs often require you to close credit card accounts when they are paid off. This will have an impact on your credit mix, which makes up 10% of your credit score, as well as your credit history, which accounts for 15%.

Alternatives for Debt Management Plans

When deciding how to handle your debt, consider the best solution for your present financial condition. Debt management is one method for dealing with debt, but there are other solutions to consider, such as:

1. Credit Cards That Allow Balance Transfers: Balance transfer cards allow you to transfer your debt to a card with a 0% introductory Annual Percentage Rate or APR. This will allow you to pay off your loan without worrying about interest. Most balance transfer cards charge fees for each balance transfer. If you do not transfer your debt to a preapproved card, you may receive a hard inquiry on your credit report.

Balance transfer cards are normally available if your credit score is in the good-to-excellent range, but they may be unavailable if your score is lower. You'll also need a clear plan for paying off your debt before the 0% intro APR term expires. After the promotional time has ended, any outstanding balance will be subject to the standard variable Annual Percentage Rate or APR.

2. Personal Loans: Personal loans provide you with a lump sum of money to pay off your debt all at once. It is similar to a balance transfer credit card in terms of debt consolidation.

If you know you'll need longer time to pay off your debt, a personal loan could be a suitable option. Personal loans typically have a repayment duration of two to seven years. Unlike a credit card, you must repay your loan at the end of the specified period, and there is no option for a promotional rate.

Your credit score will determine the interest rate on your debt consolidation loan. Interest rates on personal loans can range from 8 to 36 percent, so make sure the rate you obtain is lower than the rate you are now paying on your outstanding debt. Before applying, compare the best personal loans on the market to get a sense of what you might qualify for.

3. Bankruptcy: While bankruptcy should be considered a last choice, it is a surefire way to eliminate some or all of your debt – or to force your creditors to agree to a payment plan.

In Chapter 7 bankruptcy, you will surrender or sell non-protected assets. The funds received will be used to repay your unsecured obligation. If you are unable to manage a payment plan, this is your best alternative.

Chapter 13 bankruptcy places you on a reasonable payment plan depending on your income. Unlike negotiated payment arrangements, creditors are compelled to work with the court to ensure you can pay your debts. The method takes three to five years and works best if you earn enough to pay off some or all of your debt.

To sum up, debt management may be stressful, and finding a way out of it can be even more difficult. Fortunately, debt management methods such as the debt snowball, debt avalanche, debt management programmes, and debt settlement can help you obtain the support you require and deserve.

They are not, however, all created equal, as some tactics have more long-term negative consequences. You may possibly find that a balance transfer credit card or a personal loan is a better option. Weigh the advantages and disadvantages of each debt management approach to make an informed selection that will assist you in meeting your debt-payoff objective in the most effective manner for your financial position.

Chapter 6

Income Streams

Whether you're an entrepreneur or a full-time employee, you can benefit from additional revenue streams. With recession fears putting a pall over the global economy, making additional money can help you sleep better at night.

Diversifying your revenue streams allows you to reduce risks, identify new growth opportunities, and respond to changing market conditions.

But who has the time for a side hustle these days?

The flexibility of the digital economy allows you to pursue side hustles that fit into your schedule while earning passive money.

In this chapter, we'll go over everything you need to know about passive income, including what it is, its benefits, the many types of passive income, and more.

What Does Passive Income Mean

Passive income comes from investments, assets, or activities that take little effort to start up. Passive income, unlike traditional forms of revenue (or active income), does not require effort to earn. You are not receiving money in exchange for your time, at least not directly.

Creating a consistent source of passive income requires upfront work that will pay off in the long run. Consider it an initial investment where you put in effort and time to create the groundwork for future payments. With the appropriate investment, passive income can help you accumulate money over time and attain financial independence.

Benefits of Generating Passive Income

While earning a passive income might help you accumulate money over time, it also allows you to deal with short-term financial issues.

Let's go over the benefits in depth.

1. Helps You Earn More Money. Relying on one source of money reduces your earning possibilities. In today's market, different income streams offer several paths to financial independence. Earning extra cash provides you with a financial buffer on which to fall back if your major source of income fails.

2. Helps You Save for Retirement. If you rely only on one wage, retirement may be a long way away. Passive income allows you to contribute money to your retirement account even during economic downturns or other financial setbacks. Furthermore, because you already have an additional income stream, you will not have to rely on your savings when you retire. This ensures a comfortable, safe, and fulfilling retirement.

3. Promotes Financial Security. A side hustle permits you to expand your earnings. So, even if your principal source of income suffers a setback, you can always turn to your side hustle. According to the U.S. Consumer Financial Protection Bureau's 2022 study, 79% of Americans are concerned about their families' financial security.

Fortunately, obtaining a passive income shields you from unexpected economic shocks.

4. Promotes Work-life Balance: Earning a passive income is about more than just money. A passive income stream allows you to work on your own schedule and make time for your family or personal life without jeopardizing your income.

Striking a balance between work and personal interests decreases stress and provides you with more time to accomplish things you enjoy, improving your general well-being.

Best Passive Income Options for Building Wealth

The economy is filled with passive income options. The key to sustainability is to find an income stream that works for you.

Here are ten passive income strategies for achieving financial independence and building wealth, both online and offline.

1. Create an Online Course. Sharing your expertise with others is satisfying in and of itself, since it promotes personal growth and allows you to contribute back to the community. And, owing to the digital economy, you can now monetize your expertise by developing an online course.

The e-learning business is expanding at a constant rate. The market will be worth $166.60 billion in 2024 and $257.70 billion by 2028. And, with the internet's global reach, you're likely to find your target clients.

Here's how to develop an online course that your audience will enjoy:

(a). Know Your Target Audience: Knowing your target audience entails understanding their preferences, pain spots, and learning styles. The more you know about your audience, the better your chances of developing material that they'll enjoy.

(b). Choose a Topic: Consider topics about which you are both passionate and knowledgeable. To validate your topic, determine whether there is a genuine demand for it. Next, examine the level of competition. Once you've decided on a topic, devise a method to set your course out from the rest.

(c). Outline Your Course: Separate your online course into sections (or modules) so that students can study at their own pace.

(d). Create Interesting Content: An online course often contains a variety of file forms, including text, video, and PDF. Create high-quality information in a variety of forms to enhance the learning experience.

(e). Create a Community: Increase your following on social media and online forums. Create high-quality content to build credibility and whet your audience's hunger for your course.

2. Own a Rental Property. With homeownership rates at their lowest in 50 years (63.1%), now is an excellent moment to purchase a rental property.

However, being a landlord presents its own set of issues. To ensure a consistent income flow, you must pursue delinquent renters and fill vacancies in addition to covering maintenance charges.

Fortunately, you can reduce these risks by applying property investment tactics such as screening renters, obtaining the best insurance policy, and doing investment property analysis. Being well-prepared and informed allows you to effectively negotiate the hurdles of property ownership, transforming your rental property into a dependable and profitable source of rental revenue.

3. Invest in Dividend Stocks. Dividend stocks are shares of established firms that pay out a portion of their income to investors on a regular basis. This not only provides constant revenue, but also allows you to profit from the expansion of these enterprises. To begin, seek for companies with a history of consistent dividend payments and great financial health.

Look for dividend-paying stocks with predicted profit growth of 5% to 15%. Investing in dividend stocks can be hard. For example, a high-yield savings account may not always be the best option. However, if you take the time to learn its complexities, the benefits can be enormous.

4. Become an Affiliate Marketer. Affiliate marketing is a digital marketing strategy in which you receive a commission for recommending a company's products. If done correctly, affiliate marketing is a viable way to generate passive money online.

In fact, the amount spent on affiliate marketing is predicted to increase from $14.3 billion in

2024 to $15.7 billion in 2025. This means more opportunities to increase commissions and build money over time.

To be an effective affiliate marketer, you should:

(a). Build an Audience: A loyal following indicates that people appreciate your suggestions.

(b). Choose the Correct Products to Promote: Marketing a product that matches your audience's preferences boosts your chances of conversions.

(c). Use Numerous Marketing Channels: Consider using blogs, social media, and email marketing to deliver value to your audience while also creating potential for passive revenue.

5. Invest in Peer-to-Peer Lending. P2P lending is a debt finance service that allows users to lend and borrow money without the need for a financial institution as an intermediary.

To make passive income using P2P networks, lend money to borrowers rather than going through a bank. In exchange, you get interest on the money you lend.

P2P lending appears to be risky because it involves unsecured loans. To mitigate such risks, use a peer-to-peer platform like Prosper or Lending Club to examine borrowers' creditworthiness and provide assessment ratings to verify them.

Before selecting a P2P platform, be sure to research:

- Borrower screening and evaluation procedures.

- Loan default rates.

- Fees related to lending.

- The platform provides tools and resources to assist lenders in making educated judgements.

Diversify your investment among several lenders. This allows you to distribute risk throughout your investment portfolio while also generating long-term passive income through your brokerage accounts.

6. Launch and Monetize a Blog. On WordPress alone, roughly 70 million new posts are published each month.

Given the amount of competition, is blogging worthwhile? In one word: yeah.

In a Semrush analysis from 2023, 31% of respondents named short-form articles as the best-performing content style, while 24% named long-form blog entries.

Granted, starting a blog and consistently writing takes time and work. However, if you continuously offer great material that adheres to SEO best practices, you can earn significant traffic that you can monetise.

You can monetize your site using:

Money Pillars

(a). Subscription-based Content: Provide premium content or services via a subscription plan.

(b). Affiliate Marketing: Promote products or services using an affiliate link and earn a commission on each sale.

(c). Google AdSense: Display targeted adverts on your blog and make money based on how many impressions or clicks you receive.

(d). Creating a Lead Funnel: Use your blog to attract your ideal customers and direct them via a sales funnel where they may buy physical or digital products.

(e). Coaching or Consulting Service: Use your knowledge to provide coaching or consulting services straight through your blog.

7. Start a Dropshipping Business. Dropshipping is a business idea that allows you to sell things without stocking them.
This is how it works.
- Create an eCommerce website or register on an online marketplace.

- Find a trusted supplier and choose things to sell.

- Add these products to your store with increased prices.

- Receive an order.

- Send your order details to the provider.

- The supplier packages and ships merchandise to the buyer.

- You earn a profit.

Your chosen supplier will handle everything from eCommerce inventory management to shipment. Once you've set up an internet store, your small business will be out and running. Dropshipping allows you to tap into a large market without making an upfront commitment in inventory management.

Even after the pandemic, the dropshipping business model is growing in popularity. In fact, the dropshipping market was valued at $249.16

billion in 2024 and is projected to reach $724.26 billion by 2027.

So, regardless of your niche, you may use this business plan to generate long-term income.

8. Invest in Real Estate Crowdfunding. Real estate crowdfunding is an investing technique that allows individuals to combine their assets and engage in real estate projects. Unlike traditional real estate investing, crowdsourcing allows you to make tiny contributions.

Platforms such as RealtyShares and Fundrise allow you to invest in a variety of real estate projects, ranging from residential to commercial.

The advantages of investing in real estate crowdfunding include:

- Diversifying your investment portfolio with less capital.

- Passive income via rental yields and possible property appreciation.

- Property management and daily operations have become less of a burden.

Before implementing your business concept, conduct thorough study and evaluation of your selected crowdfunding platform's track record, the types of projects it offers, associated fees, and hazards.

9. Sell Ebooks. Self-publishing companies have enabled authors to access a global audience without relying on established publication routes.

The global eBook market is estimated to expand by $8,316.2 million between 2024 and 2027. So, this is the best time to produce and sell eBooks.

Follow these steps to make and publish an ebook:

(a). Choose a Topic: Writing an ebook, like designing an online course, requires you to choose a topic on which you are informed. Make sure the topic you choose addresses an issue. This allows you to provide a unique solution while also satisfying an unmet market need.

(b). Create Quality Content: Begin with an outline and ensure that the contents of your ebook are simple to read and understand. Proofread and revise your content to guarantee that readers receive an error-free ebook.

(c). Format Your Ebook: Formatting your ebook makes it more visually appealing to your readers. It also improves readability and makes your ebook work with a variety of reading apps.

(d). Invest in a Professionally Designed Cover: You can hire a graphic designer or build your own book cover. There are numerous book cover layouts to pick from when using graphic design programmes such as Canva.

(e). Publish Your Ebook: Many websites allow you to publish your ebooks for free. One of these is Amazon Kindle Direct Publishing (KDP). Amazon's popularity enables you to reach a worldwide audience while earning money on autopilot.

(f). Implement Marketing Strategies: After you've published your ebook, it's important to spread the word. Reach your target audience with social media marketing, email campaigns, podcasts, or collaboration with other authors.

Implementing an effective marketing strategy will allow you to enhance the visibility of your eBook over time. The higher your visibility, the better your chances of recurring income.

10. Create a YouTube Channel. With 210 million YouTube users in the United States alone, using a YouTube channel to create passive income makes a lot of sense.

However, earning money on YouTube needs more than just submitting videos. Here are some tips for being a great content creator:

Money Pillars

- Choose a topic that you are knowledgeable about.

- Create consistent, engaging, and high-quality video content.

- Responding to comments lets you interact with your audience.

- Use well-researched keywords in your video titles and descriptions to increase discoverability.

- Use YouTube analytics to determine your target audience and tailor your content accordingly.

If you have 4,000 public watch hours and 1,000 subscribers during the last year, you can join the

Money Pillars

YouTube Partner Programme (YPP) and gain access to extra income options.

Aside from the YPP, other ways to earn money on YouTube include:

- Becoming an influencer.
- Joining an affiliate programme.
- Crowdfunding your project.
- Content licensing for other artists.

You can also set up a YouTube shop to sell online stuff like t-shirts, souvenirs, and personal care products.

Final Thoughts
Creating passive income streams can greatly improve your financial status. However, in order to generate long-term assets that can help you

build wealth, you must approach financial security in a systematic manner.

Exploring the passive income concepts offered in this chapter is an excellent place to begin. Even if you've identified a profitable side hustle, you must keep up with market and industry changes. This enables you to adapt your strategies in order to remain competitive, manage risks, and grow your organization.

Whatever form of revenue you choose, having a good website is crucial. A website makes it easy to sell your items and create a unique brand identity.

Money Pillars

Chapter 7

Savings Blueprint

Saving is easier when you have a plan; use these steps to create one.

Beginning to save money can be the most challenging aspect. This step-by-step outline will assist you in developing a straightforward and realistic strategy for saving for all of your short- and long-term objectives.

1. Keep a Note of Your Expenses. The first step towards saving money is figuring out how much you spend. Keep track of all your expenses, including coffee, household products, cash tips, and monthly payments. Record your expenses using whatever technique works best for you—pencil and paper, a simple spreadsheet, or a free online spending tracker or app. Once you have your data, sort it by category, such as petrol, food and mortgage, and total the amounts. Check your credit card and bank statements to make sure you included everything.

2. Incorporate Savings into Your Budget. Now that you know how much you spend each month, you can begin to create a budget. Your budget should show how your expenses correspond to your income, allowing you to plan your spending and minimize overpayment. Make sure to account for frequent expenses that do not occur every month, such as car maintenance. Include a savings category in your budget, and aim to save an amount that is first comfortable for you. Plan to eventually save 15 to 20% of your salary.

3. Find Ways to Cut Costs. If you're not saving as much as you'd like, it might be time to cut your expenses. Determine which non-essential spending, like entertainment and dining out, you can reduce. Look for ways to save money on fixed monthly bills like car insurance or cell phone rates. Other ways to cut everyday expenses include:

(a). Use tools like neighborhood event listings to find free or low-cost entertainment options.

(b). Review recurring charges. Cancel any subscriptions or memberships that you aren't using, especially those that automatically renew.

(c). Compare the cost of eating out versus cooking at home. Plan to eat the majority of your meals at home, and look into local restaurant specials for occasions when you want to spoil yourself.

(d). Wait before making a purchase. Wait a few days before succumbing to the urge to make an unneeded buy. You may discover that the item was something you wanted rather than needed, and you may design a plan to save for it.

4. Set Your Savings Goals. Setting objectives is one of the most efficient ways to save money. Begin by examining your short-term (one to three years) and long-term (four or more years) savings goals. Determine how much money you'll need and how long it will take you to save it.

An emergency fund (three to nine months' worth of living expenses), a vacation, or a car down payment are all examples of common short-term goals.

Common long-term goals include making a down payment on a home or renovation project, sending your child to school, and retiring.

Quick Tip

Set a tiny, attainable short-term goal for something fun but out of your monthly budget, such as a new smartphone or holiday gifts. Reaching modest goals—and enjoying the reward you've saved for—can give you a psychological lift, making the benefits of saving more immediate and maintaining the habit.

5. Define Your Financial Priorities. Following your spending and income, your goals are likely to have the greatest impact on how you manage your savings. For example, if you know you'll need to replace your car soon, you can begin saving for it now. However, keep long-term goals in mind; retirement planning should not take precedence over more immediate needs. Learning how to prioritize your financial goals will help you better allocate your finances.

6. Choose the Appropriate Tools. There are several savings and investing accounts available to meet both immediate and long-term goals. And you don't have to pick just one. Examine all of your options carefully, taking into account balance minimums, fees, interest rates, risk, and when you'll need the money, to determine the best blend to help you save for your goals.

Short-term Goals

If you'll need the money soon or need to access it right away, choose one of these FDIC-insured deposit accounts:

(a). A Savings Account. A certificate of deposit (CD) secures your money for a certain period of time at a greater interest than a savings account.

Long-term Goals

Consider the following when saving for your child's education or retirement:

- Individual retirement accounts (IRAs) or 529 plans, which are FDIC insured, and tax-advantaged savings accounts.
- Securities, which include stocks and mutual funds. These financial products are available through a broker-dealer.

7. Make Savings Automatic. Almost all banks provide automated transfers between checking and savings accounts. You may pick when, how much, and where to transfer money, as well as split your direct deposit so that a piece of each paycheck goes directly into your savings account. The benefit: You don't have to worry about it, and you're less likely to spend the money. Other simple savings strategies include credit card incentives and spare change programmes, which round up transactions to the nearest dollar and deposit the difference in a savings or investing account.

8. Watch Your Savings Increase. Each month, you should examine your budget and assess your progress. This will allow you to not only stick to your personal savings goal, but also recognize and resolve issues immediately. Understanding how to save money may even motivate you to find new ways to save and achieve your goals sooner.

Chapter 8

Risk Management: Protecting Your Wealth

Wealth management is similar to being the custodian of a treasure chest, handling large sums of money for clients. Smart risk management approaches are critical for protecting this resource and assisting clients in meeting their financial goals. In this chapter, we'll look at why risk management is so important and some simple ways for keeping wealth secure.

Why is Risk Management Important?

Consider risk management to be a form of financial protection. Life is full of surprises, and risk management helps us plan for occurrences that may have an impact on our assets or businesses. Whether it's a volatile stock market, economic difficulties, natural disasters, or cyber threats, risk management steps in to preserve our hard-earned money.

Implementing effective risk management approaches is akin to having superpowers. It reduces the risk of losing money and guarantees that we reach our financial objectives. It's like employing specialized tools, such as risk management software, to demonstrate that we're prepared for anything. Furthermore, it fosters client trust and demonstrates that our investments or businesses are in capable hands.

Simple Risk Management Techniques

1. Diversification: Diversification entails not placing all your eggs in the same basket. Spread your investments over multiple types of assets, such as stocks, bonds, and investments in various locations. If one thing fails, the others may still succeed.

2. Asset Allocation: Asset allocation is the process of determining the best mix of investments depending on your risk tolerance, goals, and time horizon. It's like developing a well-balanced recipe to ensure that your money grows consistently.

3. Hedging: Hedging is similar to having a back-up plan. Use specific tools, such as options or futures, to keep your investments from losing too much value. It's a little complicated, but it helps ensure you don't lose too much money.

4. Stop Loss Orders: Stop-loss orders act as a safety net. You select a specified price, and if your investment meets that amount, it is automatically sold. It's a strategy to limit the amount of money you can lose on a specific investment.

5. Due Diligence: Due diligence is equivalent to doing your homework before making a major decision. Investigate and gather information about an investment to ensure it is a good fit. This allows you to avoid any surprises down the way.

6. Regular Review: Regularly checking on your investments is similar to keeping your car in good condition. It entails reviewing how your investments are performing, looking for any issues, and making changes to your strategy as needed.

Consequences of Neglecting Risk Management

Not paying attention to risk management is akin to embarking on a voyage without a map. It can cause major complications. Risks may go overlooked, and if you do not have a plan in place to deal with them, business may face financial losses, legal issues, and reputational damage. It's like playing a risky game without knowing the rules, putting everything on the line for short-term benefits.

To sum up, in the realm of asset management, risk management is your superhero cape.

Diversification, asset allocation, hedging, stop-loss orders, due diligence, and frequent reviews are all easy tactics that can help you keep your money secure and achieve your financial goals. It's like having a solid shield to safeguard your riches and maintain it resilient and powerful.

Money Pillars

Chapter 9

Creating Wealth Through Entrepreneurship

Starting a small business is rarely a spontaneous act—it's usually the result of deep, personal motivations that differ from one entrepreneur to the next. For some, it's a desire to escape the ceiling of salaried work; for others, it's a passion project that unexpectedly turns profitable. Whatever the reason, when you peel back the layers, one truth often remains: the pursuit of financial growth and personal freedom. Entrepreneurship offers something few other paths can—uncapped earning potential and the power to shape your own direction. It is one of the most dynamic tools for building long-term wealth, not just because of the money it can generate, but because it places the reins of financial control directly in your hands.

Paths for Wealth Creation

Creating money should be considered as a lifelong journey rather than a single event, and it can be accomplished by pursuing one of four basic paths. These paths include inheriting wealth, saving and investing, pursuing a lucrative career, or starting your own business. Each path presents unique opportunities and difficulties that influence the quantity of wealth accumulated and the time required to accomplish so.

One of the most powerful avenues to wealth growth is entrepreneurship. It is open to people of various ages, education levels, and demographics. A company's value can rise dramatically over time, resulting in the acquisition of huge wealth. However, there are hazards associated with entrepreneurship, including financial risk and the likelihood of business failure.

Wealth Creation: Start With the Ultimate Goal in Mind

Most books and articles on entrepreneurship state that the first step is idea generating. However, anyone considering beginning a new firm should first consider and define their wealth goals and objectives.

As an entrepreneur, creating wealth entails establishing a productive business that creates income for the owner while increasing in value over time. This can be accomplished by increasing profits and selling the business or shares for a large profit. It is critical to define your business expectations, such as whether it will be a side hustle or full-time, how much income is required to support your personal budget, and whether it will generate wealth beyond living expenses for future investments such as purchasing a home, funding retirement, or paying for your children's college tuition.

Once you've identified your wealth goals, you'll have a baseline for determining the fiscal sustainability of your new business idea.

Idea Generation and Validation

Developing a viable company idea entails more than spontaneous thinking or just turning a passion into a business. It entails carefully finding a market gap and comprehending potential clients' wants and preferences. The most common error a new business owner may make is attempting to sell a product or service without fully understanding the target market's needs, preferences, and readiness to buy.

Once you've developed an idea, you must validate it. Validation necessitates market research to ensure that your product or service generates enough income and profit to fulfill the entrepreneur's financial goals and objectives.

Don't be a Victim of the Fish in the Fishbowl Phenomenon

Imagine a little fish in a fishbowl. The fishbowl depicts the market in which a small business operates, while the fish represents the company itself. The water in the bowl represents the resources accessible to the business, including capital, talent, and customers, all of which are limited by the size of the fishbowl.

Interestingly, the fish does not realize he is in a fishbowl. Looking through the glass, the fish perceives the entire room as his habitat, despite the fact that his universe is defined solely by the boundaries of the fishbowl. A fish can only grow as much as its fishbowl allows, and a tiny business can only sell as much as its market requires. If the fish grows past the confines of its bowl, it may require a larger environment to flourish.

Similarly, a company may need to assess whether the proposed business idea is actually limited to a local market or if there are opportunities for other markets and broadening its products in order to continue growing.

The fish in a fishbowl analogy effectively depicts the problems and opportunities that an entrepreneur must examine before starting a new business. Like fish, firms must adapt to their surroundings, manage resources intelligently, and deal with the consequences of market limits. Understanding the fishbowl effect allows potential business owners to better assess the viability of their ideas.

Aligning Business and Personal Wealth Goals

The great majority of micro-small business owners don't have a business plan, and many don't even have well-prepared financial predictions. Some take satisfaction in "flying by the seat of their pants." However, data on small business failure shows that a well-structured business plan is critical to long-term business success and sustainability.

However, for the entrepreneur to profit from the firm, the business plan must be in line with the owner's own financial aspirations and ambitions. The plan outlines your business objectives, strategies for accomplishing them, and the resources needed. A strong business plan contains market study, financial estimates, and an operational plan.

Balancing Business and Personal Financial Health

A critical component of establishing financial success through entrepreneurship is ensuring that the business can scale and grow beyond generating only enough income to support the owner's family. Any business's growth and scaling should be the product of careful planning, including a capital budgeting plan. Every year, a number of small firms go bankrupt due to unplanned or unanticipated growth. My father once told me, "A chance is only an opportunity if you are in a position to take it."

Obtaining finance is critical for any organization to meet its growth goals. Capital readiness is planning for and addressing the financial health of both the firm and the owner. If the owner's financial situation is unstable, it might have a detrimental impact on the financial health of the business, and vice versa. Finally, acquiring a business loan requires rigorous capital planning and administration to accomplish the required growth and success.

In a nutshell, entrepreneurship is a significant tool for generating money. However, it is only effective when idea generation results in an economically viable business model, which is backed by strong business planning, capital acquisition and structure, managed execution, planned growth, and reinvestment.

While the trip is difficult, the potential benefits are great. Understanding and using these essential concepts will allow you to leverage the power of entrepreneurship to generate significant riches.

Chapter 10

Legacy Planning: Protecting Your Wealth for Future Generations

Legacy planning is a critical component of financial management that extends beyond the individual's lifespan. It secures the transmission and maintenance of riches for future generations. Legacy planning is a deliberate method to manage investments, assets, and estates that ensures a smooth transfer of wealth from one generation to the next.

Comprehending Legacy Planning

Legacy planning entails multiple steps, including drafting a will, establishing trusts, managing estate administration, and addressing tax ramifications. The primary goal of legacy planning is to preserve family resources and values so that future generations can benefit from them. Individuals can ensure that their legacy thrives long after their lifetime by properly structuring their assets and using successful techniques.

Preserving Family Wealth

One of the primary goals of legacy planning is to protect family wealth from potential risks and dangers. Effective asset protection techniques, such as forming trusts or storing assets in secure institutions, can protect money from creditors, legal battles, and other threats. Individuals who preserve family assets can provide a sound financial foundation for their heirs and beneficiaries.

Minimizing Tax Implications

Tax preparation is an important part of legacy planning since it can have a substantial impact on wealth transfers. Individuals can reduce tax liabilities and optimize wealth distribution to beneficiaries by implementing tax-efficient techniques and structures. This may include using tax-advantaged accounts, gifting tactics, or philanthropic planning to reduce the estate's tax burden.

Facilitating Succession Planning

Effective legacy planning is especially important for family-owned businesses and organizations. Succession planning is an important part of legacy planning since it entails making clear plans for leadership changes in order to maintain the business's continuity and long-term survival.

This may entail grooming successors, building governance structures, and developing exit strategies to ensure a smooth transition of ownership and management. Individuals that prioritize succession planning can protect their enterprises and wealth for future generations.

Educating Heirs and Beneficiaries

In addition to asset preservation and tax planning, legacy planning should prioritize heir and beneficiary education and empowerment. Providing financial literacy, value-based education, and responsible stewardship training can help future generations handle their inherited wealth responsibly. Individuals can ensure that their legacy lives on beyond financial wealth by instilling financial discipline and ethical ideals.

Seeking Professional Guidance

Legacy planning is a complicated process that involves professional assistance from skilled consultants such as estate planners, lawyers, and financial specialists. These professionals may give bespoke solutions, personalized guidance, and complete services based on your specific requirements and goals. By collaborating with competent experts, you may confidently negotiate the complexities of legacy planning, protecting your money and preserving your legacy for future generations.

Legacy planning is critical for individuals who want to preserve their riches and values for future generations. Individuals can ensure that their legacy lives on after they pass away by implementing appropriate asset protection, tax planning, succession planning, and education methods. Embracing legacy planning principles ensures that families will have continuity, stability, and prosperity for future generations.

Conclusion

In the closing pages of "Money Pillars," we are at a crossroads of opportunity. The trip we've taken is more than simply about money; it's about redesigning our financial future. As you close this book, remember that abundance is a daily reality, not a faraway ideal. Each chapter served as a stepping stone, unveiling the secret keys to prosperity. Now, armed with knowledge and determination, you're ready to move forward. So go ahead, accept the money pillars, and watch your life change.

www.ingramcontent.com/pod-product-compliance
Lightning Source LLC
Chambersburg PA
CBHW071920210526
45479CB00002B/492